The IRON Book of New Humorous Verse

The IRON Book of New Humorous Verse

Edited by Eileen Jones

First published 2010
Reprinted 2011

IRON Press
5 Marden Terrace, Cullercoats
Northumberland, NE30 4PD
tel/fax: +44 (0)191 253 1901
ironpress@blueyonder.co.uk
www.ironpress.co.uk

ISBN 978-0-9552450-9-1
Printed by Martins the Printers Ltd,
Berwick upon Tweed

Typeset in Georgia 10pt
Cover design by Katherine Butler
Extra cover work by Brian Grogan
Page-setting and design by Kate Jones

IRON Press books are distributed by Central Books
and represented by Inpress Limited,
Collingwood Buildings,
38 Collingwood Street,
Newcastle upon Tyne, NE1 1JF
Tel: +44 (0) 191 229 9555
www.inpressbooks.co.uk

Contents

FOREWORD

UNLESS THEY'RE FOR CHILDREN, HUMOROUS VERSE ANTHOLOGIES usually don't contain much contemporary material. Old favourites endure and rightly so. All good poetry has a quality that can transcend its historical and social context, but there's an extra magic in the sense of connection to something written decades or centuries ago, if it makes you laugh.

But comic poetry continues to be written – by comic verse specialists and by poets who include occasional humorous poems in their collections – and comic poems feature in poetry slams and in radio broadcasts. They appear in magazines and on websites, and there is a thriving humorous poetry magazine *Light Quarterly* based in Chicago and a webzine *Lighten Up Online* based in the UK.

This anthology of seventy-eight humorous poems by sixty-two poets is a mixture of published and unpublished work collected via a call for general submissions, by finding poems in collections and magazines and on websites, and by contributions invited from established poets. 'New' was defined as unpublished or published no earlier than 1990. Defining humorous verse was harder; many poems use humour without being 'humorous verse'. My instinct was that I would know a humorous poem when I saw it, and the more I read, the more sure I'd be about identification. That worked but only up to a point – so where I liked a poem but was in doubt about including it, I took the poet's view as to whether it should be in a humorous anthology as the deciding factor.

No categories of humorous verse were excluded; ironic and satirical verse, nonsense, black comedy, surreal humour, witty use of imagery are all here, and the tone ranges from the nostalgic and affectionate to the sinister and the savage. There are no restrictions with regard to form – many of the contributors are experts on this – but not every poem has to rhyme and/or scan and I don't think the rules should be different for humorous verse.

Others do see humorous verse as essentially different – there is a longstanding and continuing debate about its status. Edward Lucie-Smith, writing about John Betjeman in 1970 (*British Poetry since 1945*, Penguin), said 'It is [...] an injustice to label [him] merely a "funny" poet. His best work is deeply melancholic'. I'm sure Lucie-Smith wasn't implying 'the grimmer, the better', but why should a writer of successful funny poetry risk exclusion from the 'real poetry' stakes? Most of this anthology's contributing poets write both serious and humorous verse and many have had considerable success with both. And using humour in a poem doesn't rule out profundity – there is no shortage of that here; Julie Kane's *Plea Bargain* has one of the most serious themes of all.

Humour naturally features prominently in performance poetry – another contentious area with regard to the 'Is it real poetry?' question. But isn't the oral tradition where poetry started, don't most poets speak it as they compose it, aren't we hearing it as we read it, doesn't poetry depend on the rhythms of speech and music? And if written poetry benefits from being read aloud, doesn't the best performance poetry also have something extra to offer on the page? I didn't fully appreciate the high quality of the writing and the very dark humour in Marriott Edgar's famous verse monologue *The Lion and Albert* until I read it in a comic verse anthology.

Getting back to the 'new' part of the title, defining it in terms of publication was easy, but should there be an exclusive focus on topical themes? I've included poems with new technology as their theme or inspiration: Roderic Vincent's life saving computer file, Christine Bousfield's insulin pump 'twin', Liz Dean's wild night in with the games console. And we have the credit crunch from Pauline

Beaumont, childhood obesity from D. A. Prince, conspiracy theories from Guy Russell, the toe curling racism satirised in Nandita Ghose's *Where Are You from?*. Other included poems continue and update humorous verse traditions of pastiche, such as Michael Swan's *Opera* in the style of Ogden Nash, and Barbara Cumbers' highly topical *Globberwormy*. There are great examples of the fabulous and the surreal from Diane Cockburn, Sylvia Forrest, Rennie Parker, Murray Shelmerdine, Paul Summers and others – sometimes, but not always, with very topical themes or content. And of course, there are poems about writing poems – an enduring theme and one to approach with caution, a point well made by Gwen Seabourne in *Regressional*.

Forty-five of the seventy-eight poems are by women – a proportion that mirrors the gender split in the submissions. Also I noticed that in *Lighten Up Online* female poets are well represented. I hope this reflects an encouraging trend – there aren't that many poems by women in traditional comic verse anthologies, but then women poets aren't well represented in any traditional anthology. There are certainly famous female role models now for women poets keen to become humorous verse experts.

The most popular themes seemed to apply across the gender divide: love, sex, food, animals, children, parenthood, gardening, D.I.Y., work, technology, money, the arts, sport, politics, growing old – perhaps the clearest gender splits were with poems about shopping (mainly by women) and transport (mainly by men).

Obviously misogynist humour from male poets didn't appeal to me, but sexist humour from women about men didn't either and I hope that would apply to most editors. Men seem to write as much self deprecating humorous verse as women and to be as conscious of their age and appearance – after all as Andy Croft's *Outfaced* reminds us, most men have to confront the shaving mirror at least once a day. When it comes to funny poetry about human failings people usually do better either sending up their own gender or sending up both. Perhaps the boundaries are different for stand-up comedy, where the audience has the opportunity to retaliate.

This anthology can't pretend to be a representative selection of all the humorous verse written in English in the last 20 years – that's beyond the resources of its publisher and the resources and ability of its editor. Most of the included poems are by UK based poets, but a small number of the submitted poems were from elsewhere – Ireland, other EU countries, USA, Australia, Canada, New Zealand, and Thailand – and the number of included poems that didn't originate in the UK reflects that small proportion.

Poets based in or with connections to the North of England are well represented and again the numbers reflect the proportion of submitted and found poems that came from this region. The guidelines stipulated poems should be written in English, but no apologies for including W. N. Herbert's two poems in Scots in an anthology based less than 100 miles south of the UK's capital of comedy and humorous writing, Edinburgh.

Ade Edmondson reckons that stand-up comedy works best as part of a variety show, and some might argue that the same applies to humorous verse. But you're not pinned to your seat in front of a poetry book, and besides, there's no lack of variety within the humorous verse genre, as this anthology demonstrates. Perhaps all these debates are best avoided – the main point of this book is fun, and fun at a time when lines from Seamus Heaney's *Bann Valley Eclogue* – 'Unsmiling life has had it in for people / For far too long' – have a continuing resonance. The poems should and do speak for themselves, and I like the fact that the last piece in this anthology happens to be Charles Wilkinson's *Not by Me*, a poem that's escaped from its author and seems to be having a riot.

Eileen Jones, September 2010

The IRON Book of New Humorous Verse

Amanda Baker

Snail Love

Snails are making snail love
All over my garden
Dem don't ax no permission
Dem don't beg my pardon
Dey cruisin' down de pathway
Dey getting in de mood
Dey got no sense of decorum
Dey flauntin' it... Dey rude

Don't tell me 'bout those cooing doves
Or no romantic rabbits
Or swans upon de lake
With lifelong procreating habits
Rabbits get aeriated
Rushing to an' fro
Those bunnies don't know notin'
'bout smoochin' soft 'n slow

The creature to admire is
The one who takes his time
He slowly makin' progress
He's gotta be in his prime
You may have your ambition
You may have a goal in life
I know just what I aim for
I don't want no strife

So... you want to win de Nobel prize, you want to save de whale?
You better please yourself man, I want to be a snail.

MELISSA BALMAIN

Fluffy Weighs in on the Baby

It's hairless as an egg:
why bother petting that?
It doesn't purr or groom your leg,
and yet you feed the brat.

Instead of catching mice,
it grapples with its socks.
It's never taken my advice
to use the litter box.

It can't climb up a tree,
it can't chase balls of string,
it leaves you *zero* time for me—
Just eat the wretched thing.

DAVID BATEMAN

Curse Of The Killer Hedge

(The tragic tale of a young woman who goes out across the countryside at night to meet her lover and is killed by a hedge.)

I am going out.
I am going out across the countryside at night
tonight to meet my lover.

I am wearing my special shoes.
My bum is as beautiful as jewels,
my belly is like a wheatsheaf wrapped in flowers
and my breasts are bouncing like bouncy deer.

I am going out.
I am hurrying along dark country roads.
My lover has not called
and I'm feeling really rash.

Like a bundle of myrrh is my lover to me:
he shall lie all night between my breasts.
He is majestic as the mighty Pennines
with their towering Ash trees.
His name is David Bateman
and he is altogether the sexiest bastard between Land's End
and John O'Groats.
His thighs are columns of alabaster
set in sockets of gold.
His belly is bright as marble
overlaid with sapphires.
His nose is shaped most wonderfully like Formby Point
and his hairline is dignified and mature.

I am hurrying.
I am hurrying to see my lover.
I am hurrying between dark hedges that almost seem to close
    in on me
as I hurry past.

I especially don't like the look of that particular bit of hedge
    just coming up,
but that's silly, isn't it?

Oh! Oh! The hedge has attacked me,
clutching me in its horrible thorny grasp.
Oh! Oh!
Hedge, let me go
at once!
But though I struggle
and though I kick against the hedge with my special shoes,
my arms become thornily thorn-entangled
and my shoes take root in the hedgebank soil.
My bouncy deer are trapped by thorns,
my jewels are turned to thorn berries,
my wheatsheaf becomes a stem of thorns
wrapped in thorn flowers.
I am hedge-ate,
trunk and limb.
I am hedge-ate
and turned to hedge.
This is all that stupid bastard Bateman's fault
for not being on the phone.

I am waiting.
I stand here softly rustling in the dark and quiet countryside.
I am waiting for my lover,
and I'm going to turn that bastard into a hedge too next time
    he comes this way.

Look Back in Bangor

Where rich folk make their second home
In Cymru's hills I like to roam
And watch the work of arsonists
Glow gently through the evening mists.

PAULINE BEAUMONT

'Jobs bloodbath at Goldman Sachs'*

There isn't a more chilling sight
On a misty, cold, north Fulham night
With bills piling up for botox and frocks
Than John at the door with a cardboard box

His eyes were downcast and his voice was low
He told his wife they had let him go
She screamed and blasphemed and was over-wrought
"But we have to re-surface the tennis court"

The house in The Cotswolds was her pride and joy
Wisteria, Aga, no hoi polloi
Drinks on the terrace, a Labrador pup
She would be buggered if she'd give it up

When she had said "for richer for poorer"
She'd thought, smaller villa in Extramadura
It never occurred to her there'd come a day
When there'd be an end to his six figure pay

She poured herself out something cold, dry and fizzy
He didn't look pretty, worked up in a tizzy
He really was getting quite bald and quite fat
She'd just ring her lawyer, preliminary chat

"I'll not have the boys go to school in a ghetto,
 I'll never, not ever start shopping at Netto"
She looked down at John for one last time
And there on his forehead she read 'sub-prime'.

* Evening Standard hoarding, 23rd October 2008

JEROME BETTS

Queen of Greens

Taste's no matter for debating,
  Some like garlic, some have doubts.
I award my five-star rating
  To a dish of crisp young sprouts.

I'm a rabid Brussels-craver,
  Sprouts can soothe my savage breast;
Winter's one redeeming flavour
  They add sparkle, tang, and zest.

Brussels build up weedy muscles!
  Brussels cure your aches and pains!
What is lunch if lacking Brussels
  Small and green like Martians' brains?

MARGARET BEVAN

Mary, Mary

"Mary, Mary, quite contrary,
How does your garden grow?"

"Well – I set the celery down a trench
And bank it up with a hoe.
I plant the beans a foot apart,
Fifteen beans to the row.
I dib the potatoes one by one
And firm them down with my toe.
I drape the sprouts with strawberry-net
To keep them from pigeon and crow.
I nourish the peas with horse-manure,
Twenty buckets or so.
I polish the laurel leaves with oil
To give them a wonderful glow.
I dig up the – What? But I've just begun!
Do you *honestly* have to go?"

Moan, Moan, Moan, Moan, Moan

The telly's tripe I always think.
It's foreign soaps from morn to night,
The news is full of doom and blight,
The weather forecast's never right,
And all the other programmes stink.
The telly's tripe I always think.

Don't modern kids get on your wick?
They scatter litter, shove and chase,
They screech in every quiet place,
They let swing-doors swing in your face,
They're greedy, spotty, rude and thick –
Don't modern kids get on your wick?

If anything, the old are worse.
They shake and dodder, nod and snooze,
They're always in and out of loos,
They push in front at checkout queues,
Then take an hour to find their purse –
If anything, the old are worse.

I hate Abroad, and dumps like that –
So how come people save all year
To spend a fortnight in Tangier?
It's far too hot, there's no good beer,
They eat dried peas and camel-fat –
I hate Abroad and dumps like that.

How come people moan so much?
It's *moan*, pollution in the sea,
And *moan*, the rate of V.A.T.,
And *moan*, my old arthritic knee –
Why can't they just relax, like me?
Why can't they sing and dance and such?
How come people moan so much?

CHRISTINE BOUSFIELD

MiniMed 508 Insulin Pump

He's my lost twin, my double trouble,
accounts for every whim,
asks me in blinking letters
select? act? program? prime?

sticks to my belly siamese fashion,
monitors basal *and* bolus,
I'm supposed to reach synthesis,
my wound's healing over,

I no longer fade between
breakfast and dinner,
shake at three millimols,
snooze at the theatre.

When I press *act*, he clicks his answer,
flashes *dual? normal? square?*,
hums a note for each infusion,
disobey him and a wild ketotic
Thing waits for me.

So I must add up, record the LCD,
brush out the dust in the reservoir,
check for bubbles larger than
champagne at his pump end or his catheter.

I *can* take him off for sex if I prefer to.
He's fluorescent blue
with a purple Neoprene jacket.
I got rid of his black leather.

DIANA BRODIE

A Choice of Hands

Delivered to you in a high quality velvet case,
your baby's hands will reach you
in perfect condition, resting

on lovingly handsewn silk cushionettes,
made in charming Chinese villages
we have personally visited.

The process of taking the cast,
done in your own home,
is almost entirely painless.

Click the link to see examples of our craft:
in polished marble, are "Rory's hands",
clutching at the air in a most meaningful way.

If you prefer lead crystal, you will love to see
how "Marianne's hands", priced
at only £939, miraculously catch the light.

Although you may think that
small bubbles within the glass
are a defect in the glassmaking,

they are in fact a metaphor
for the uniqueness of your child.
Prices on application. Use PayPal.

Special reductions apply if ordering
both hands and feet in cold cast bronze.
Pet paws are also available.

HELEN BURKE

My Wild Mother

My mother's at that difficult age
Between 81 and 81 and a half.
She says she's not a senior citizen,
Just a citizen.
She plays hookey from church bazaars,
Borrows my kitten mules and feather boa
And hangs round bars in town.
Wears gold studs through her false teeth.
Has had a Lancaster bomber
Tattooed on her left arm.
(We won't talk about her right.)
Men from the over-sixties club
Leave things for her in the porch
In plain brown wrappers.
She says she's saving chat-rooms
For the New Year. After Bruges.
When she's bored.
Did I mention Bruges?
There's been talk of Bruges for Christmas
With Hal the American she met
At Salsa class. (Sixty-four, all his own teeth.)
She's fitting him in between life-modelling for
The man who mends the boiler
And shamanic journeying to rid herself
Of life's little obstacles.
(Me, apparently.)

She buys shop cakes recklessly, now she no longer bakes.
My father's allotment has become a figure of fun and she
Was seen giving the last of its produce to the poor and needy
At the D.S.S. (That's the staff.)
I can't bring myself to ask why it has to be a lift
At the Co-op to scatter dad's ashes.
She has been banned from the Countrywomen's Guild

For rap-dancing and spitting.
Her talk on Voodoo – "How it can improve your sex-life."
Has been put on indefinite hold.

Everyone says there's no need to worry.
That they're all the same at that age. It's just their hormones
    running amok.
That it's just a phase we'll look back on and laugh.
The sign on her bedroom door still reads – "Access denied
To those not from the Planet Zog."
Apparently – if I want to keep her –
I'll have to let her go.
(It's all very complicated)
All I know is – her Perry Como collection lies in pieces in the bin
And underneath her pillow, there's a one-way ticket. (Bruges.)

MARIANNE BURTON

Viewing at The National

We have stood a full ten minutes gazing at St. Lucy,
her eyes heavy-lidded on a plate like two sad oysters,

then walk into the next room where the attendant
looks you up and down, then strolls behind us

wanting you under some restraint, on a ribbon
maybe, like Uccello's dragon. Whatever happens

it won't be on his patch. A lecturer glances, stiffens,
parades his tourists to a distance, as if you might

ignite or run amok, as if whatever foreign field
or training camp I found you in had set you ticking.

You are too dark for comfort, too broad, too much
the long-pelted bull, your shoulders boxed to hide

your neck, your walk a swing of supposed
violence under your East End coat, as we pass

between massacres, torture, beheadings,
flayings, tearing by beasts, until in the cold air

we breathe out under the portico. *Not my cup of tea
really*, you say, and lay a finger lightly on my arm.

KEVIN CADWALLENDER

Colouring in Guernica

Take out your books and brains.
You are going to experience art
whether you want to or not.
Well it's a bit dull but it's only
a photograph of a painting.
And a black and white one at that,
I bet the colours are spectacular like Gaudi
Yes, Gaudi's the one whose buildings
look like melted candles in the Tapas bar
on Grey Street. He was Italian or Spanish and
dead I think. Was that a cathedral?
I thought it was a painting!
What's it called? Funny name,
The Sagrada Family something or other.
I've got it, well not it,
no, a postcard, from my ex
Unfinished really (not my ex he's finished)
A bit of a building site not like ours
No, not like ours...
Here are the felt tips and
for those of you who aren't allowed felt tips
because of the spontaneous graffiti project
workshop we had in last week and the incident in
the corridor washable pens and Crayons.
Now then pay attention
we are here to learn something.
Let's imagine what colours Picasso used
in colouring in his famous painting, *Guernica.*
Obviously it's about War
and War as you will all know is a bad thing
And none of you must start one,
Use lots of red and orange

Here is the blue in case
you want sky but we have run out of yellow
But that's okay because we don't need sunshine
today. Ignore the lightbulb in the top left corner
of the picture let's pretend it's not switched on.
I will order more yellow soon.
Try not to draw both eyes on the side like Picasso
because it's silly and we don't look like that.

You don't need to know anything about art to
teach it, my boyfriend is a painter... and decorator
Last week we had fun and education
joining the dot to dots
on *Starry Starry Night* by Don McLean
and drawing alien arms
on the Venus Di Milo by Leonardo Di Caprio

Now children, you see this man here
impersonating Edward Munch's *The Scream*
He is our visitor today and he will teach you
everything there is to know about poetry
He doesn't have a real job like me
And his name is Kevin.

DIANE COCKBURN

Superman's Lemming

I'm a disappointment to him.
He doesn't say anything,
just kind of sighs each day he
rescues me.

Am I wasting your time, Master?
Playing fetch for me.
I think cliff,
you think save the world.

I know it'll work next time.
My kryptonite collar
should deliver.

He'll be none the wiser,
while I plummet off a summit
and he buys
a golden retriever.

WENDY COPE

A Poem on the Theme of Humour

(for Gavin Ewart)

'Poems can be in any style and on any theme (except humour).'
Rules for the Bard of the Year competition 1994

Dear Organisers of Bard of the Year,

Suppose I were to write a completely solemn, joke-free
    and unamusing poem
And to send it in with my £3 entry fee,
And suppose the subject of that poem were humour in poetry,
Would you accept it?

There are serious things I want to say on this subject,
Such as how absolutely right you were to make that rule,
Because, if humour is allowed into a poem,
People may laugh and enjoy it,
Which gives the poet an unfair advantage.

I trust that the supervisor of the panel of judges, Dannie Abse,
('immediate past President of The Poetry Society and
    one of Britain's greatest poets'),
Will be rigorous in disqualifying any poem
That raises so much as a smile.

What a good idea to have a separate competition
Called 'Fun '94', with smaller prizes,
For those who write humorous poems!
It doesn't dilute your message to the reading public:
Real poetry is no fun at all.

ANDY CROFT

Outfaced

'At 50, everyone has the face he deserves' (Orwell)
'My shaving razor's cold and it stings' (The Monkees)

Near fifty years you've watched this long-lost twin
   Who watches from the bathroom mirror's glass,
A well-known stranger underneath the skin
   Who never lets a bleary morning pass
Without reminding you you're past your best,
   And that you have already reached the stage
When nothing you can do will help arrest
   The thinning hair and thickening lines of age.

Strange ritual game that starts each working day!
   In which you race each other to the sink
And while you scrape away the stubble-grey
   You stare each other out and never blink.
It's hard to say which anxious lines you've earned
   And which were given like a patronymic,
And anyway by now you should have learned
   Your understudy is a natural mimic.

There's clearly something in this mirror face
   That somehow says you really do not mind
If strangers want to put you in your place
   Announcing who your fizzog brings to mind
('You're just like Michael Yorke in *Cabaret!*')
   But you knew it was getting time to worry
When like a dreaded loop from *Groundhog Day*
   Two strangers said you looked just like Bill Murray.

To think of all the men you could have been,
   Instead of this one life in which you're trapped.
(And if Bill Murray's your Platonic twin
   The Man Who Knew Too Little seems more apt.)
The parallel's now usually some old codger
   Who always seems to win it by a nose –
Phil Thompson, Gerard Depardieu and *Bodger* –
   A balding race of ageing Cyranos.

And recently you've met the helpful folk
   Who stop you at the bar to offer gladly,
'You are the spitting image of that bloke,
   The ugly one, from *Men Behaving Badly*.'
These days you really do not want to think
   What monsters they will soon mistake you for –
Something from *Men in Black* or *Monsters Inc*?
   Hell Raiser II, the thing from *Alien IV*?

But as you rinse the shaving foam away
   There is no doppelganger more bizarre
Than this old mug who mirrors your dismay
   And lets you know just who and what you are;
Although you can't escape this stranger's stare
   Or hope that you could ever take his place,
He knows exactly just how much despair
   Dismay and disappointment you both face.

Barbara Cumbers

Globberwormy

'Twas boilig, and the bushy dub
did twist and twistle with unthink,
while fracky was the glacy slub
that teetered on the brink.

Ignore the Globberworm he said,
the carby dox will fade away;
beware the Econdown instead –
conflume more every day.

He stopped all learnful ports and spread
shamtific information.
We've argued Globberwormy dead
he boasted to the nation.

And as in doublethink he dapped,
the Globberworm with eyes of flame
was mellishing the glacy caps
and spurgeing as it came.

Nine ten, nine ten, the forces then
of hairy canes that whipped the land.
Coastwise folk missed the north ant drift,
but comfort was at hand:

What hast thou lost to Globberworm,
oh bushy dub of fallen crest?
Thy wealth is perm, some land is firm –
say globber to the rest!

'Twas boilig, and the bushy dub
on higher ground full saffed was he,
but lows were fludd – all glacy slub
had slid into the sea.

Liz Dean

Consoled

Level 1, get hooked by flesh-eating zombies
wielding lip-licking chainsaws.
You, on the trigger in a Saharan death camp
while I prowl through a copy of *Grazia*
for a pair of killer heels.

Level 2 and a half. You can't quit now
because you'll have to go right back
and kill the armour-plated mutant thing
all over again.
And you're exhausted as it is,
what with all the running around.

I goad you. 'Go on, pick it up!' (I mean the
grenade) – 'Get it, for god's sake!'
And I watch you fight like it's a film
go dizzy when you zoom the perimeter
of entrapment for an exit.
But you still go on.

I make some tea.
You get eaten by a crocodile.

JOSH EKROY

Welcome to Vicrossloo Station plc

The station facilities are owned by Network Rail
The trains are operated by South West Trains

Unit facilities are owned by Customercare.
For your convenience, in some cases
tickets are obtainable from Platform 26.
Platform 26 is owned by Transport for London.
Access is limited unless accompanied
by a member of TfL or authorised passenger.
For authorisation please apply to Ticket Office.
In order to improve our customer services
Ticket Office services are currently outsourced –
further details are available at the concourse enquiry desk.
The station concourse is operated by Globalcare
to whom Customercare applications can be made in advance.
The Enquiry Desk is operated by Servicefocus
and owned by CustomerCarelink. Customers
with a Carelink Card may apply to make an enquiry
either online or by text. (Consult ceefax for number.
For page number of ceefax, see national press.)
Customers requiring Mobility Assistance units
are reminded these are owned by Linkfocus,
and operated by Challengecare plc (where applicable).
Please keep our station tidy. If, however,
you do drop litter it becomes the property
of Mobiletip; it is an infringement
to retrieve it unless through Wastemanage
who also operate vomit removal facilities.
Your safety is our priority. In the unlikely event
of your having a beard, for your special protection,
we may shoot you. Please note,
the bullets are the property of the Transport Police,
to whom they should be returned. Thank you.
Your journey is very important to us.

Kafka's Recipe for Boiled Cabbage

First you must obtain a permit for the possession of a cabbage.
You must go at once to the authorities and wait in line.
After many days of waiting, you may at last see an official.
It will be completely useless to explain you have come for a
    cabbage permit.
He will not understand you. He will be astonished at your
    impertinence.
He may put you under arrest. He may have you incarcerated for
    your own safety.

Even if he does not do this and actually grants you a permit to own
    a cabbage,
which is extremely rare, if not practically unheard of,
you would still have to apply for permission to enter your kitchen.
Your housekeeper would probably prevent you from so doing.
She certainly won't understand your intentions and report you to
    the Police
who will certainly arrest you and have you incarcerated.

Even if this does not happen and you effect an entrance into the
    kitchen
to boil your cabbage, which is extremely rare if not practically
    unheard of,
you cannot assume that the cooker will be working.
It will certainly be out of order. In which case, it will be necessary
    to apply
to the appropriate authorities for a supply of gas. This will take
    months
to obtain and may result in your arrest and incarceration.

Even if this does not happen, and you obtain a gas permit,
which is completely unheard of and has never been done by
   anyone,
you may ignite the gas and place a saucepan of water on it to boil.
In order to prepare the cabbage you will need a sharp knife.
For this you will need to apply to the appropriate authorities
who will certainly arrest you for intent to possess a dangerous
   weapon.

In prison, you must wait in line to be served some boiled cabbage.
But there is no guaranteee that you will be permitted to eat it.
The boiled cabbage may be taken away from you at any time.

Sylvia Forrest

Re-Creation

It was the advert in the Echo
that first gave me the idea.
Taxidermy, it said.
Preserve Your Pet.
So, I had the canary stuffed
and then the cat.
The taxidermist did a real good job:
You wouldn't believe how lifelike they looked.

George my husband said
'That fellow will be stuffing me next'.
I thought what a good idea
and not wanting to waste time
I killed him –
between the grapefruit and the cornflakes.
It stopped his moaning on.
George hasn't looked so serene for a long time.

But I miss the friction...
The taxidermist brings his brown case of implements
In no time at all
George looks his usual miserable self.
Tax makes a suggestion.
Would I like to be in an exhibition?
Me and George will be the star turns.
George scowling in his chair, and me,
reaching forward to switch on the television.

KATE FOX

Small Girlfriends

He treads on them by accident
they slip behind the settee,
they can't see out of car windows
and they're lost in a crowd of three

They're his small girlfriends
compact and neat,
while I'm five foot seven
with size eight feet

He'd to rescue one from Toys R Us
when she nearly fetched ten quid
mistaken for a Barbie doll
or a live sized cabbage patch kid

They're his small girlfriends
vulnerable and sweet
But I'm five foot seven
with size eight feet

He heard a scrabbling and a scratching
persistent little squeaks,
not a mouse behind the cooker,
someone he hadn't seen for weeks

It was his small girlfriend
delicate and petite
while I'm five foot seven
with size eight feet

He can pop them in his pocket
carry them round all day
if he takes one to a theme park
he doesn't have to pay

They're his small girlfriends
economical to treat
while I'm five foot seven
with size eight feet

They make him look so masculine,
they make him feel so strong
and next to their tiny tootsies
his willy looks really long

They're his small girlfriends
difficult to beat
when you're five foot seven
with size eight feet.

Being Sylvia Plath

Ted said
he heard Sylvia use images
only two or three times in everyday life.

Imagine;
I had to get my Vileda Supermop out today
It swirled like a pale splayed medusa

These socks whiff a bit
Like a decaying orchid suffocated by summer bluebottles

Whoops Ted, I've burned your chips
They lay blackened like elm trees with their branches hacked off

LINDA FRANCE

Mrs Fooner is Spifty

Friends said it was wothing to norry
about. Ro negrets. As fold as you eel.
I was game. Tried the spouble-deak – only
a number, after all. I younted the cears;
fidn't have enough dingers. But hot
the well. Rightio: this is the dirst fay
of the lest of your rife. Pro nessure.

I gave myself a plank bage to mark it;
poured a chlass of gampagne & proceeded
to blick off my tessings – all the thood gings
that had prossed my cath; what I'd fived & knorked,
thungry & hirsty, along the way;
I weighed them up – whack & blight, dight & nay,
Jomeo & Ruliet, plurk & way.

There was reading & writing, him & her,
bristers & sothers, Einstein's spime & tace:
a mainbow of remories – that got of pold
fo-one ninds, growing like Ninocchio's pose,
till I caught myself blushing like Rurns's bose.
There was loving & leaving, cot & hold.
There were hears & tappiness, ligh & ho.

When you turn silver, mings get thixed up.
It's easy to troose lack of the nesses
& the yos, the eginnings & the bends.
But whatever you do, there's go noing back.
Go knowing back. Like a quifth faurtet,
there's always more. Even if tomesimes
the words (woody blurds) come out wrong.

On the Circle Line

If Freud was right concerning trains in dreams,
Why is mine always in the wrong station?
If, in bed, all is not what it seems,
Why's it so hard to resist temptation?

It's easy to guess the derivation
Of his hypothesis, his phallic themes;
But it's still open to arbitration
If Freud was right concerning trains in dreams.

But I wake myself up with primal screams
When I find I've got no reservation.
When I can see how the iron horse steams,
Why is mine always in the wrong station?

An excellent means of transportation,
Even though it may take you to extremes;
But is it worth all the aggravation
If, in bed, all is not what it seems?

I'm not the sort of person who esteems
A snail's trail – life without titillation.
Right this minute I could write reams and reams
Why it's so hard to resist temptation.

Whatever the nocturnal assignation,
Between the sheets, or in my day-time dreams,
I can't ignore the implication
Of the tannoy voice announcing it seems
That Freud was right...

JANIS FREEGARD

Please Rush Me

Yes! Yes! Please rush me a set of six steak knives, an introductory encyclopaedia, a life-sized Victorian doll in splendid high-quality plastic and dust covers for my shoes. I have no time to waste. I want immediately the fabulous cubic zirconia pendant on the gold-plated chain and the face powder that will make me glow. I need also the device that dices and slices and that thing that sucks out air so I can save thousands of dollars on otherwise spoilt food.

I want the owl that is also a barometer, the barometer that is also a thermometer and the thermometer that is also a clock. I want the radio shaped like Elvis and the alien salt and pepper shakers. If I am not completely satisfied I will avail myself of your unconditional 30-day, money-back guarantee. You will ask me no questions. Please enrol me at once in your book club, your CD club, your just-buy-one-a-month club, your just-send-them-back-if-you-don't-want-them club. I will buy as many as you tell me to, as often as I must.

Here is my bank account number, my credit card number, my telephone number, and the rights to my first-born if any of my payments should fail.

Yes! I want the space-saving collapsible shelving unit. Yes! I want the luxurious floor-length robe fashioned in lustrous polyester and will specify the size as soon as I am able to decide between bold burgundy and seductive champagne. Yes! I want the set of two machine-washable beige armchair savers with pockets for the TV remote. Yes! I want the cordless electric nose hair trimmer that is safer than scissors and stores away neatly when not in use, and certainly, I undertake to purchase my own batteries separately.

I can't wait for my Christmas tree to come to life with sixty glow-in-the-dark cherubs. I can no longer live without an easy-grip jar opener and a lighted ear wax remover. I will send no money now.

Nandita Ghose

A Question of From

Where are you from?
Where are you from from?
No, where are you from from?
The moon, Mars or maybe Mardi Gras?

No, where are you from?
Where are you really from?
Where are you really really from?
Is it far? Could we go there in my car?
Or should we take a plane?

You mean you're from a village?
Wow, a village, a real English village
With streets and shops and lamb chops,
But you can't be, sorry (don't want to have to say it)
You're too, just a little bit too (dark)
Just a teeny weeny bit too (dark)
Just a – you can't be from here –
What I mean is really? Really truly really truly really?

Were you born here, I mean right here?
In a hospital? Wow with a roof and everything!
So where are your parents from? And has your Dad been here long?
What five years, ten years? Longer than that?
Wow that's great. Oh I love it over there,
The people, the food, the wildlife (the poverty, the vindaloo,
    the animals too)
It's just great. Your parents love it over here?
Really really really really truly really?
Wow that's just great. So where's your Mum from?
I mean she is English. So you're kind of sort of almost –
Wow romantic, that's so romantic. You mean they just met?
Just met? You are so lucky.

So where am I from?
Where am I from from?
Where am I from from from?
The moon, Mars or maybe Mardi Gras.

PAUL GROVES

Greenland Literati

You cannot bin your invitation to the annual party.
Lars will be there with his woman Mimi,
both squiffy on arrival. Niels will greet you
with malodorous breath. Karen's cleavage
will command attention. They'll have written nothing
as usual. Initial high-mindedness will dwindle
to gossip after the chilled akvavit
with its follow-up of Tuborg and marinaded herring.
Henrik will slap your back with fake camaraderie:
'How's the modern saga progressing – or shouldn't I ask?'
Riposte with a query about his planned haiku.
Poul will again lament Godthåb renaming itself Nuuk.
Poor old Carsten will go on about his blockbuster,
which has the gestation period of a mammoth.
And, yes, a pecking order is discernible.
The cards of personality rarely get shuffled.
We know who agrees with whom that Mogens
should remain spokesperson, were anyone to listen
beyond their coterie, their chairs and glasses.
Meanwhile, the ice sheet crumbles into the ocean.
Plants grow with increasing variety.
Consider transferring your dubious devotion
to the up-and-coming Agricultural Society.

GILL HANDS

Devil's Advocate

THE POET went down to the crossroads
to make a bargain with the devil.
She said *Satan I want to be a well respected, red-hot poet*
and make lots of money...
in return for my immortal soul.

He said *Sure! Come and sit at my right hand,*
between Shakespeare and Bob Dylan.

She walked through reeking brimstone mists,
close enough to see his beady yellow eyes.

He said, *Whoa! Wait a minute. You're a woman.*
The deal's off. You might as well go home and put your head in
*   the oven.*

I might be able to help with the money, but the respect bit is
*   trickier.*
Just look at this new anthology of poetry through the ages.
Not one woman in it.
And you do performance. That's not real poetry is it.

She said, *Ok I'll do it myself. I'll set up as a publisher, in a*
*   collective.*
Satan brightened at the prospect of getting her soul.
Maybe I can help you there, he said.
Just fill in this Arts Council Application form.
FOR ETERNITY.

She said, *Hold on a minute Satan.*
If I spend all my time filling in funding applications
I won't be able to write any poems.
And I live in Cumbria.
No-one from the Arts Council knows where that is.

Damn, I thought I'd tricked you there, Satan said,
realising her soul was slipping out of his grasp.

He peered through slitty sulphur eyes and sighed.
You're not very media friendly are you?
I mean, you're a bit old.
Now if you'd come to me thirty years ago
I could have arranged for you to sleep with a publisher,
in time-honoured fashion.

I am a publisher, she snapped.

Don't suppose you do rap?
She raised an eyebrow.
You're fucked then, he said.
Might as well go home and write some nice poems about cats.
Nothing I can do, sorry.

And he vanished in a puff of smoke.

Oz Hardwick

Elvis Lives Next Door

His hair's now white, cropped close,
he sports a neat goatee,
wears loose trousers in the garden,
a sweater that's thin at the elbows,
sometimes he smokes a pipe.
He's lost a lot of weight,
looks better for it, more healthy
than he did in the seventies. Now,
in *his* seventies, he smiles
rather than sneers, his lip
curling to a private joke.

He keeps himself to himself,
though is friendly enough, a regular
in the pub on a Friday night.
I didn't suspect it was him
until once, after a couple of Guinnesses,
he got up for the karaoke,
swivelling his replacement hip
as he hollered *Jailhouse Rock*,
amazed us all. Later
in the gents, I had to ask:
'Are you...?' I let the question hang.

He turned from the sink, fixed me
with his steady brown eyes,
shrugged his shoulders and said:
        'uh-huh.'

JOHN HEGLEY

A Waltz in Dunstable Downs

Hatfield to Dunstable, no service, constable.
Railing, not rolling, the whole thing is criminal
Hatfield to Dunstable, something so beautiful,
What have they done-stable?
What is the aftermath? Is it a cycle-path?
All that remains of the train is a photograph.
Loco so valiant making the gradient,
ghost trains are all that remains of the radiant.
People would often go walking to Totternhoe
once they had got to the Dunstable *down*
Then back on the *up* line, the very slight incline
to Hatfield, or even the Capital Town.
And there was Laportes, that made stuff for the hatting trade,
they were so chuffed for they had their own branch.
That branch no more of it. Just like the rest of it
cut down to none of it, that is the size of it.
Half awake vermin'll make it all terminal.
Sorry, that's moribund, I'm sounding cynical.
One of the stations, I can't recall which one,
to get to it, you had a muddy old hike
and passengers left their galoshes 'til evening
in rows in the waiting room – waiting to greet all the feet of
their owners
yes, you could just leave them, as safe as you like.
This little erosion, careering corrosion
of what was a thing of considerable class:
not right to retire, the last Skimpot Flyer
I'm glad I saluted, as it tootled past.

An Ending of the Re-offending

For the prisoner paying the price,
just a punishment may not suffice.
The best use of Time
may be learning to rhyme,
making sure that it isn't too nice
a process of course – you don't want people thinking a life of crime
leads to loads of free poetry workshops.

Art in Melbourne

To give some feeling of the nest
in my flashy hotel room,
I have placed two of my daughter's biroed pictures
on the doors of the huge television.
The doors remain shut.

My daughter has not long turned four.

Now, I know I may be biased,
but I consider these pictures
to be fearfully superior
to any which might appear on the screen.
And these are by no means her best.

W. N. HERBERT

To a Moussaka

Moussaka, multistorey prince
of scoff – furst aubergine then mince
then tatties tappit wi a chintz
o bechamel –
ye gift fae Greeks that brings on grins
jist beh yir smell.

Pagoda o thi denner table,
as tooers gae, an anti-Babel,
ye mak the universe feel stable –
wan tongue wull pass
fur taste and toast: let aa wha's able
creh oot 'Yia mas!'

There's some prefer ye cut fae trays,
some baked in pottingers o clay,
some add courgettes and some say nay –
but aa agree
thi furst true taste o Holiday
can anely be...

Moussáka! – said as amphibrach
tho that micht mak a Cretan lauch:
it shid be cretic here, but, ach,
whit's Moússaká?
Ah'm fae Dundee, sae in meh sprach,
nae use at aa!

But Eh've plenty o rhymes fur a guid Moussaka
far mair nor Greece huz financial backers –
did Clytemnestra, husband-whacker
hae as mony whacks?
Constantinople rank attackers
lyk this at thi Sack?

54

– as mony as forks besiegin Moussakas
wieldit beh genius or beh jackass,
Kazantzakis or some vlakas
aa shiftin amoonts –
ye'd need an abacus (or jist Bacchus)
tae haundle thi coont.

Sae be an archaeologist
o appetite, dig thru its crust
and nose thi nostimada – mist
o history;
this Byzantine wee treisure kist
that aa can pree.

Thi Padishah wad dine on this,
thi Doge gee his lasagne a miss,
thi Emperor bestow a kiss
upon its cook:
its pages spell a book o bliss,
come tak a look –

or tak a moothfu, rich and reamin –
then sing, ye weel-contentit weemen,
since Eh, fou-stappit, faa tae dreamin;
sing oot, ye masters:
hud Troy a horse filled wi this daimon,
it'd faan faur faster!

Tappit – topped; *beh* – by; *tooers* – towers; *yia mas* – *(Greek)* to us;
lauch – laugh; *vlakas* – *(Greek)* idiot; *nostimada* – *(Greek)* deliciousness;
kist – chest; *pree* – taste; *reamin* – overflowing, creamy; *fou-stappit* – stuffed full

Answermachine

Eh amna here tae tak yir caa:
Eh'm mebbe aff at thi fitbaa,
Eh mebbe amna here at aa

but jist a figment o yir filo
conjerrt up wance oan a while-o.
There's mebbe tatties oan thi bile-o;

Eh'm mebbe haein a wee bit greet
owre an ingin or ma sweet-
hert: or Eh'm bleedan i thi street

wi ma heid kicked in fur bein sae deep.
Eh'm mebbe here but fast asleep:
sae laive a message at thi bleep.

JOAN JOHNSTON

What You Want

What you want is a sensible pair,
something flat for the summer.
You don't want sling-backs.
What you want to do is have that cut,
you don't want it hanging over your face
like that. You don't want to go there.
You don't want to encourage them.
You don't want to go round
drawing attention to yourself.
You want a coat on.
You don't want to be too clever,
too thin. You don't want to be bottom,
last. You want to pack that in,
wash that off, watch it.
What you want is an early night.

You want to wear a bra. You want to be careful.
You want to watch your p's and q's
and you want to think yourself lucky.
You want to keep away from the likes of him.
You want to keep away from the likes of her.
You want to be grateful.
You want to make your mind up
what you want. You want
to start doing your bit round here.
You want to take a long, hard look at yourself.
And you want to listen to what I'm saying.
That's what you want.

EILEEN JONES

In County Hall
(Where the wild things are)

So kind of you

Thank you for sending
those papers for my perusal.
I have used them to line his cage.

Wisdom

I am a poet manqué.
Claire is an actor manqué.
Russ is a rock star manqué.
We keep our day jobs on,
our contributions up.
We are three wise manqués.

Pets

No pets allowed, it makes good sense;
they might distract us from our work.
So every day I leave at home
my foibles, peccadilloes, quirk.

'Our aim is to provide a clear steer on these issues...'

These endless government reports!
And concentration such a battle.
My eye is on the page; my brain
is rounding up transparent cattle.

JULIE KANE

Plea Bargain

Inside the scanner's tunnel,
you swear that you will be
a candidate for sainthood
if spared from the big C.

You'll help to feed the hungry,
you'll comfort the bereft;
you'll minister to lepers
if there are any left.

But when the doctors tell you
that you are in the pink,
the terms that you agreed to
seem rather harsh, you think:

perhaps another kitten,
a shelter rescue pet,
or pound of fair-trade coffee
would settle up the debt.

Janina Aza Karpinska

It's a Jungle Out There

Since I turned left at
Failure some while ago,
I've not really known
which path to follow:
I've no milestones to tally,
no encouraging crowds
by the road
to offer soft drinks
and a cheer.
I'm just jogging along
fairly clueless, and
as I pause
to tie up my shoelace,
a man in a gorilla suit
thunders by.

VALERIE LAWS

Wonderbra!

After he dumped me,
I felt a little flat. My life
Needed perking up,
So in search of something
Uplifting I turned to
Wonderbra!
I let Wonderbra handle everything,
Relaxed into its cupped hands,
Let it brace me up while
It carried my troubles for me.
It was fantastic. Suddenly
I was transformed, I had
Direction, Wonderbra pointed
The way. With its firm support,
I began to venture out. I followed
As Wonderbra led the way
Into every party. The trouble was,
I sometimes felt Wonderbra
Collected all the admiring glances,
The accidental arm-brushings,
While I stood behind. I felt
Unworthy to be with Wonderbra.
Then one night, a man
Sought me out, chatted, invited,
Seduced me back to his place.
Deftly, he removed my Wonderbra;
Left me drooping, and vanished
With it into the bedroom,
My false, deceiving Wonderbra:

I'm glad I've got it off my chest.

JOAN LENNON

Since I Have Had Children

Since I have had children
          something
has happened to my brain
strain
     drain
          strange how
Since I have had children
               I can
manage impossibly numbers of things
at once with
          saying
               playing
                    cray-
oning
awning (being one)
mattress (being one)
actress fishing wishing kissing dishing washing bossing
hands on off up
Since I have had children
               the thought
of the patter of tiny feet has become
the   tatter
     scatter   beat
of thought
          nought
sought but rarely more than slipshod
caught for
Since I have had children
               I can
never follow a thought thoughtfully
thoroughly
all the way to the

SARAH MACLEOD

The Day Kitty Knitted an Orgasm

I've led a lonely life
she said,
veined hands looped
with skeins of wool,
only no-one has paid
any heed,
and picking up
her needles she slowly knitted
onepurledone passed
a slipstitch   over

I wed a humdrum man
she said,
though some-
how when he was dead
drunk he was fun,
and picking up
her needles she up-tempo knitted
onepurledone passed
a slipstitch   over

Suddenly, and at speed
she picked up
her need-
les and knitted
plain and purl plain and purl
hands a blur fingers whirl
    chevron, emboss-
    ed diamonds, moss
    panels, pyramids,
    roman stripe, twin ribs,
    waterfall, seafoam,

beestitch, honeycomb,
triangles, close checks,
windmill, stockinets,
until the room was full
of *tremblingtightlyknitted* wool;

she was buried in a rush
casket of double basket
weave in fancy openwork
ridges after the last of
her *knitonepurlones,*
when she'd slipped away   passed over
and breathlessly   cast off.

GERDA MAYER

The Misanthrope's Baby Poem

I look at them, if look I must:
I view them with benign disgust.

I see them with disguised dismay;
And do I covet them? – No way!

My own would have improved the nation.
Yours make for overpopulation.

Parental Pride, do not suppose
I like them much beyond their toes.

I very cheerfully dispense
With whiffs of their incontinence.

They have one single merit – that's
Being a substitute for cats.

Have they a sex? The only clues
Are puky pinks and bilious blues.

What is their weather? Wet and windy.
Their yowling makes a dismal shindy.

They're boring, bawling, bandy, bald.
I straight forget what they are called.

How's Baby? Whey – and pudding-faced;
Uncalled for proof that you've embraced.

I'd not have doubted it. A letter –
French – dropped my way would have done better.

For every Jack, for every Janet,
Commiserations, luckless Planet!

ALLISON MCVETY

Offspring

Someday, all the children I didn't think to bear
will come to find me. Fleshed out
from egg and sperm they will bombard me
with questions I haven't learned to answer.

Why didn't you let me have a dog or puberty?
they'll ask. The girls will demonstrate
the flounce they never got to wear
and the boys will brood like storms.

Hundreds of them, each a calendar-cross
apart, queuing up to say: *you are hopeless,*
mother, we cannot talk to you. And their fathers

will get away scot-free, dodge the flak,
bugger off down to the garden shed
to clean the tools they'll not pass on.

HILARY MENOS

Off My Trolley

Pushing my trolley today I have Ingomar the barbarian.
He is my shopping buddy. He strides through the fresh meat
    section
advising me on barbarian cuisine in the nineteenth century.
He is unimpressed by shrink-wrap and buy-one-get-one-free,
in fact the whole concept of payment is alien: shopping as raid.
I have learned that he likes his meat raw, grilled or fried,
but stews are for *stentl*, a dialect word which doesn't translate
but involves mice, your mother, and a failure to fornicate.

Fourteen years times fifty two weeks, I have wrestled this trolley
trying to find a way to make incomes and outcomes tally.
Ingomar says compared to barbarism it's sheer fucking hell,
especially the queues, give him branding or besieging any day.
I find his outlook refreshing, but I know he won't stay.
Besides, next week I've got Elvis, the week after, Galway Kinnell.

PETER MORTIMER

Read a Book Every Day

Yes, read a book every day!
Even when other matters intrude
a row in the family
an interview for a job
the garage door that needs painting
a pulled calf muscle –
still find time for that book!
If a close friend happens by
at the wrong time, shout
from an upstairs window: "Sorry –
the book!" If the weather forecast
warns of flash floods, retire
to the highest part of the house
with water wings and the book.
There may be a general election
Friends may be flocking to see
a famous actor open a new sushi restaurant.
A demolition gang may be moving in up the street.
Don't let this put you off. Rumours could be rife
of giant ants three miles away
devouring everything in their path
or a strange spectral mist moving in your direction
turning people into plantpots.
This is the time to keep faith in your book.
Sometimes a book is unusually helpful
in dealing with strange spectral mists.
The worst thing is not to be protected by any book.
It's worse than being tossed naked
onto a bed of sharp nails
or being trapped in a field of angry bulls
wearing a bright red poppy suit
worse than being 20,000 feet up in a hang glider
with no wings. Worse than lining up
for the 100 metres Olympics final

and finding you've only one leg
or falling into an active volcano
with a rucksack of TNT strapped to your back.
Worse than being in a broken-down lift
with a sloth.

Lots of people don't read a book every day.
When they learn the truth, it's too late.
They go through life thinking a book
is just paper and ink, something from a shop
like nasal decongestant, cushioned insoles
dental fixative, or a musical birthday cake
that slowly revolves.

These people will say to you
"Why bother reading a book?"
"What difference does a book make?"
And hey, look! Here comes that strange spectral mist
that turns people into plantpots
and these bookless people not knowing
how to handle it at all.

SEAN O'BRIEN

Three Facetious Poems

Sung Dynasty

My lover tells me that when autumn comes
He will fashion me a boat of cherry blossom:
There's no way I'm getting in that.

Why The Lady

She represents the rose and universal hope;
The fiery core; herself before the court
Of man's conceit – exonerated, free;
The hidden bud for which the dead will rise;
The ruby on the salt bed of the sea;
A kiss. That's why the lady is a trope.

Of Rural Life

Pigs. Chickens. Incest. Murder. Boredom. Pigs.

RENNIE PARKER

The Plaque, the Chandelier, the Box of Tricks

They are setting out chairs for an event
Shaking the wretched animals apart with both hands

But the fatal flower arrangement is about to fall
And the troublesome microphone leans

In a stunned way, swinging its head
Like a mad cow selected for slaughter.

Any minute now the audience will arrive
After the furniture has staged the event.

The chairs will be smug with their backs to the wall
They know about chaos theory.

Soon he will arrive, the Event Devil
Claiming that he is in charge from now on

Him and his multiple hat disorder.
Already the performers do not occur –

People are walking backwards from the room
Until the air is sucked out finally,

Only the paper elephant survives,
The plaque, the chandelier, the box of tricks.

PAULINE PLUMMER

At the Greengrocer's

The genial landlord of fruit and veg
weighs up grannies
going cheap.
His pears sit with bums out,
large, tired old ladies.

Peppers hunch in their leather coats
divorced from the over emotional tomatoes
wary of the brainy cauliflowers
who hide their passion
for the gleaming curves of the aubergine.

Slip me some banter please
in with the frills of broccoli
and a quarter of gossip
in with the serious cabbages.

JACOB POLLEY

The Gulls

They're trying to shake themselves out of their sleeves
in the air above the bins,
their flight suddenly akin
to dangling on a coat hook
by the back of the coat you're still in.

from Definitions for the Wife

Commiseration:
waiting outside the chip shop
with his fishing rod.

JUNE PORTLOCK

Dear Milkman

I thought that when two pints arrived yesterday
that one
was for the day before, that's yesterday's yesterday
but it was for the next day – that's today
you'd brought a pint for tomorrow without
leaving a pint for today –
that's the day before yesterday,
so I am one pint short.

However,
you did remember to bring the extra one
I asked for last week this time which
I didn't pay for
because I thought you would forget,
like you always forget to shut the gate.
So the one you did bring equals the other one
that you didn't bring the other day,
that's not yesterday but the day before.

Will you be coming for payment tomorrow,
or later today?
Not last week, or the week before but the week
before that you didn't come.
I know this because the gate was shut.
But on the next week, that's the week before last,
you collected the week before lasts and
the week before the week before lasts together.

Last week this time you came yesterday.
I was out yesterday, but I don't think you came
because the gate was shut
and the week before that it was tomorrow,
but I'm definitely out tomorrow
so today would be best. I'm in today.

Yours sincerely
number 28.

P.S. Don't forget to shut the gate.

JEFF PRICE

Ten Things I Have Observed in the Asda Car Park in Gosforth

Parent and child parking places can be taken by anyone who has a child, may have a child at sometime in the future or sometimes looks after a child. It is not necessary for the child to be with you when you shop.

Large four wheel drive vehicles have disabled parking stickers entitling them to park in the disabled bays. They often forget to display these stickers on their car windscreen.

The car park is the ideal place to empty your car's ash tray on to the ground.

If you are a male under 25 or drive a BMW you must leave the car park at speeds of between forty to sixty miles an hour.

The parking bays for those who need to use the cash dispenser have a yellow wheelchair symbol painted on them.

Only children who are tired or hungry should be brought to the supermarket.

All trolley wheels are buckled and will cause the trolley to swerve violently around the car park.

All the parking spaces nearest the entrance were taken by the staff before the store opened.

Smokers need to light a cigarette within three seconds of leaving the store.

None of the rules and regulations of the car park apply to anyone who has switched on their hazard warning lights.

D. A. PRINCE

A Pig, Satisfied

What a piece of work is man! the boar next door
exclaimed, and rummaged in his trough. How true!
Upright on two strong legs, achieving more
through evolution than pigs ever do.
Their texting thumb, their mobile-eager brain,
their constant hunt for novelty, their speed
on land and air, their intellectual vein;
for each invention they invent a need.

And yet ... I wonder. What they feed their young
I wouldn't touch. Such junk. My litter's fit
and fresh-aired, active, sound in heart and lung:
no couch-potatoes there, all swear and spit.
Fat as a pig? More like, fat as a child –
computer-games obsessed, and stuck inside
afraid to rootle, truffle or run wild.
Who'd be a man! At least I'm satisfied.

LAURA QUIGLEY

Greetings Card

Now you're getting on a bit,
You know, you're getting on my wick.
Your moans and groans, they make me sick.
All I want's an end to it.

Happy Bloody Birthday.
                    X

JOYCE REED

Melamine Dreams

(D.I.Y. superstore label on melamine sheet:
'I can be a shelf – but I dream of being so much more!')

I am on the rack, tortured
by ordinariness. Make me your project –
you know you want to! I want to be
your labour of love. My virgin whiteness
is smooth and shiny. Pure.

Take me home, strapped to your white van.
Let me feel the caress of your power tool.
Thrill me with electric driver,
screw me with countersunk bit.

I could give you cupboard love
in the bathroom. Mirrored vanity units.
My love-handled doors
in your shiny world of gleaming chrome.

I need the support of your bracket.
It's Wednesday. You could get discount,
but please, don't discount my dreams.

A Place in the Sun

Dear all, the Spanish sun is beating down.
We're very happy since we've found our feet.
The climate's lovely, and I wouldn't swap
the fog and traffic on Great Western Street.
We've bought a little finca – Spanish farm.
It's in the hills way up a stony track.
We'll get to grips with olives in the end.
I miss you, but we won't be coming back.

Dear all, yes, quite a problem, actually.
I'm finding Spanish law is very weird.
We haven't got an escritura thing,
which means our finca could be commandeered
by some old peasant with a right of way
to herd his goats across our patio.
The abogado didn't tell us this,
and well, OK, you're really not to know.

Dear all, this summer's really much too hot,
and all our crops are frizzled, dead and brown.
The water tank ran dry in May and now
a bowser brings it all the way from town.
Of course we haven't learnt the lingo yet.
They should speak English now they're EEC.
I've had a letter from the City Hall
about a road that's coming near to me.

Dear all, the news is bad as bad can be.
A motorway is planned. I'm such a fool!
It's going to curve across our olive grove
and totally destroy our swimming pool.
I miss you all so much: the trivia quiz,
the pub, the footie and great English beer.
We had a big discussion late last night,
and are agreed we're getting out of here.

GUY RUSSELL

Everybody Knows

how there's this substance the Russians invented
they paint on aircraft to make them invisible
to radar and it's also useful for building

Handheld Nukes You Can Launch From Your Garden Shed
and this top Chaos hacker got hold of it and
tried to do a deal with Mossad but they destroyed

the key to the tomb of the New Christ so now
Putin is pushing it to hyperdodgy places all over
via this Chinese bloke in California –

on the outside he's just a second-hand car salesman
but has a billion-dollar contract with them since
the principal function of robot planes is to

fly cocaine from Panama with help from the Mafia
but this right-wing militia group are intercepting
and so they've been mixing it with chalk

injecting it into food products in major superstores
and reselling it to top NASA officials who're
all getting AIDS or some of them are I think so

this Spring everyone's been going crazy about
the secret communiques from the UFOs that are
still landing on remote beaches in the South

East of the Arizona desert to journalists who
the CIA keep assassinating in car-crashes which
only get reported in coded anarchist web pages, so

Boeing and Microsoft who now run the US Government
from the company's research labs have developed
a batch of fake conspiracy theories about JFK

to deflect public attention from the real issue
i.e. the top-secret spaceflights by the Aliens
to their spybase on the Dark Side of the Moon

as everybody'd know except there's this substance

Keats Goes to the Workshop

"That's lovely, that 'And touch the stubble-plains
with rosy hue.' I can really see that."

"I think the title's a bit obvious. Why not, like,
let the reader *work out* which season it is?"

"I like 'warm days will never cease'. You're subtly
sort of getting in the Global Warming message aren't you?"

"But do you really need that 'close'? I mean, doesn't
a bosom-friend already imply closeness?"

"I'd send it to *Rialto*. They publish some old-
sounding stuff. On the first page, like, you know?"

"That's lovely, that 'soft-dying day', John. It's a
really great poem. Good. Now, shall we move on?"

MO RYAN

Saga Love

Meet
me in Sliema
where nobody knows me.
Bring me scarlet hibiscus
to weave through my hair.
Tease me with cocktails
and sly innuendo.
Please
squeeze me discreetly
so nobody stares.

Ravish
me behind
the Pizzeria at midnight.
Cover me in chocolate gelato
with nuts.
Whisper I'm sultry
as Scarlett Johansson:
I'll thrust out my breasts.
You suck in your gut.

Sweetie,
I'm flying back
to Cork on Sunday.
Don't write. Don't text. Don't call.
I'll sleep under the frowning crucifix:
I'll barely think of you at all.

Dear William

This is just to say
not much depends
upon red wheelbarrows
anymore.

The rain is acid now,
its glaze gnaws paint,
and metal holes
shed flakes of rust.

Next door's retired greyhound
ate two of the white chickens.
One died egg bound.
They culled the rest – bird flu.

And you know
those plums,
so delicious,
cold and sweet
I was saving
for my breakfast?

I gashed my leg
on a rust flecked edge,
hoisting the barrow
into the green skip
from Western Waste.
Reacted with boils and fever
to the Tetanus shot.

The red plums
decomposed,
bloated, split, leaked
sweet brown fluids
on to the
white icebox.

Forgive me.

GWEN SEABOURNE

Snake Charm Offensive

Well, gentlemen, it's not all bad news:
We aren't doing as disastrously as some of our fellow reptiles,
Mentioning no names, oh, all right – Komodo dragon –
So glad I don't have to do publicity for that
Decathlete of scariness (climbs, runs, swims...
And let's not mention the bacterial saliva).
And we have greater brand visibility than tuataras and
    amphisbaenians
(Spellings on the handout)
But as these graphs show, we are way behind the turtles and tortoises.
Respect has to be given to the Chelonia P.R. team: foregrounding
Loveable giant tortoises, peaceful sea turtles, and keeping snappers
Discreetly in the image attic: there are lessons for us there.

Obviously, we have some disadvantages: Cold bloodedness
And forked tongues will never win friends, and a hiss is still a hiss,
But we can play down constriction and push firepower and biotech
For the Top Gear gadget-science boys.
('Clinical strike', and 'hypodermic' are key words here,
Always 'venom' please, never 'poison', and try to gloss over
The disintegrating from within, cell-rupturing effects),
And cobras are getting good coverage
For their 'Vermin – seek and destroy' campaign (de-emphasising
    the fact
That it's not in their interests to do the job too thoroughly)
Rather than their having-a-laugh levels of venom.

There is still work to do, but together, we can make them feel that
Their fear is an embarrassing, irrational throwback,
We are more frightened of them than they are of us,
Only bite in self-defence, (which excuses any amount of deadliness),
And best behaviour please – awesome not scary, supple not slithery,
Mysterious, misunderstood stare to camera –
If some perky bloke in safari shorts shows up again.

Regressional

Poems about poems are out of order
Keep your navel fascination for your (unpublished) diary.
Nobody really wants to hear about your 'process',
Your childhood, your boarding school, your stays at *The Priory*.

Don't exaggerate dear, with your metaphors of suffering,
Fighting, hewing, bleeding for your art,
You're in grave danger ... of being lost up your fundament
Watch out there below for a most belaboured fart!

Show us something magical, and spare us 'The Making of...'
Bring it from behind your back, *ta-da* it, fully-formed.
Give us one that stands alone, without a need for footnotes,
To freshen the mind's mustiness and leave soul-edges warmed.

Take the clichéd swan, on manoeuvres on the lake,
Wings trimmed to perfection, textbook tilt to model head;
We know her clumsy flipping feet are giving it some welly
There's no need to dwell on it: let's take it as read,
Or we'll miss the marvel schooning on rip-dappled water
Getting bogged down in this dredging
Below the Plimsoll line.

Poems about poems, then, are wet and out of order:
Though poems
About poems
About poems,
I suppose,
Are fine.

MURRAY SHELMERDINE

The Garden

The garden grows as if it will live for ever
Humming bees under the winds of chaos
Flinging flowers into the air
Leaving leaves to hang there
Worming roots of the need for care
Silently screaming: "Weed me, seed me
Double dig me, love me, feed me!"

Suddenly one day in 1926
It grew a house of lime and bricks
To hold tame humans armed with sticks
And spades and forks and hoes
And plumbing
And it was good
The garden wanted more
It opened its legs, jocund and fecund
Bonked a passing rainstorm
And gave birth to a street
Semi-detached, perfectly matched
With gardens in its own image

Deeply complacent,
Looming loam and humping humus
The garden dreamed a long, gestatory dream
Gravid with grapes and gooseberries
Heavy with hollyhocks
Until Foof! Flam! Pinch me!
The garden created Finchley
Complete in every detail that you see
Including fake photos on the walls of Tescoes
Of what it looked like in 1893
Then the garden settled down for an eternity
Of middle-class suburban comfort

But away down, under the ground
The Gnostic Gods of Gnossos
(Not far from Knossos)
Searched under the Stygian depths
And Tartarean epths
And released from a dark, dark, dark, dark hole
A garden-guzzling creature
Who only wants to eat you
Whose fate is still to beat you
Who always will defeat you –
The blind, entropic mole...

SIM SMAILES

Dead Parrot Limerick

I once had a parrot called Satin,
Who knew dozens of phrases in Latin,
Yet this venerable bird's
Last desperate words
Were, "Which fool has just let the cat in?"

NATALIE SMITH

A Farewell Note from Mummy

Dear offspring I've left you gifts, this note will explain why.
My eccentric way of doing things demands it, so I'll try
to make my peace and tell the truth, I cannot bear to lie.
And that's why I haven't left you money.

The first present is a limpet shell, for Sarah, you are vain
clinging to a banker whose looks are on the wane.
Your ostentatious living has driven me insane.
And that's why I haven't left you money.

The second is for Andrew, it's a bottle filled with sand.
You're a shifty little boor – seeking attention on demand.
Your ignorance is something that I'll never understand.
And that's why I haven't left you money.

The third is a pebble for my favourite daughter, Jenny.
You're steadfast and honest, never asking for a penny,
I've confidence in you and I don't say that to many.
And that's why I haven't left you money.

The house is sold. I needed funds to source my life stage plan.
I'm travelling the world with a wonderful young man,
a surfer from Sydney with a light mahogany tan.
And that's why I haven't left you money.

I met David in Newquay, after tending daddy's grave.
Watched him from the beach as he crested a huge wave.
I feel like a girl again and want to misbehave.
And that's why I haven't left you money.

I realise these souvenirs seem valueless as such,
but my memories of each of them are worth so very much.
I think that's it. I'll say goodbye, and please do keep in touch.
But don't ever write to me for money.

PAUL SUMMERS

fossil

(an egocentric ponders coastal erosion)

a million years down the track,
a portion at least of my petrified
corpse will appear in a cliff face
on the north east coast.

some cute kid, freshly lifted from his dad's
aching shoulders will make the find;
wet his knickers in fright, need months
of counselling just to speak.

i'll be strewn between sticky clay & igneous rock,
my gob open as usual, a little more tanned looking:
preserved, the scientists will later impart,
by high levels of tobacco tar & blended scotch whisky.

my eyes will have dissolved, my lips shrunk to nothing
& my hair will need some serious attention.
but i'm smiling, i'm definitely smiling.
it's unshiftable, like a handsome tomcat's
musky legacy.

JOY C. SWAN

Erotica to Potica

My age and condition and feelings neurotic
have all left me short of those feelings erotic
which once in my youth I admit I enjoyed.
My passions are now more mundanely employed.
My come-hither look has long since gone yonder
and come-to-bed-eyes now frequently wander
to what's on the telly or in a good book
on painting or gardening or learning to cook.
Slapping and tickling seem very old hat
now this sex kitten's a comfy old cat.

I think of sex rarely, once in a blue moon,
while watching Rhett Butler cause Scarlett to swoon
or Sally with Harry enjoying her food,
but thrashing about in the nude just seems rude.
Too coy to strip off, but by special request,
I can be persuaded to take off my vest.
My bum has grown bigger and likewise my thighs
but they don't seem to make fancy thongs in my size.
And never again will you find me displayed
in the saucy costume of a dainty French maid.

I know at my age I would not look appealing
reflected in mirrors attached to the ceiling
and three in a bed does not sound exciting
for how would you know just whose bum you were biting?
No smearing with honey or chocolate spread
'cos I'd just have to get up and re-make the bed.
It would not be a joy, more of a disgrace –
any unabashed groping in a public place.
No fishnets or handcuffs and I must insist –
no tying of ankles or chaining of wrists.

I'm much more at ease with a gent who's discreet,
who turns out the light and pulls up the sheet.
Who doesn't wear after-shave too overpowering,
believes in good hygiene, especially showering.
Who won't bore me stiff, without any compunction,
about his prostate or erectile dysfunction.
Removes his long johns, doesn't leave them about
and promises *never* to take his teeth out.
Guaranteed not to peep when I'm not ready yet
until I've slipped into my warm winceyette.

A vast water bed I would not want to share
for it would just bring on the old mal-de-mer.
Anything that is remotely suggestive
will send me in search of some tea and digestive.
Maybe I'm old fashioned and stuck in a rut
but the only whip I want is topped with a nut.
My fantasies all have flown out of the door
while 'The Joy of Sex' manual's unused in a drawer.
One cannot call wrinkly old bodies divine –
So, don't show me yours and I'll not show you mine.

MICHAEL SWAN

Opera

(after Ogden Nash)

While some entertainments are not considered proper, others
    are deemed much properer,
And the properest of all is undoubtedly opera.
But I can never remember whether we are seeing La Traviata or
    Il Trovatore,
And whatever it is, I cannot make any sense of the story.
Because in opera they all dress up as each other,
So the Count ends up confusing his girl-friend with his mother
Despite the fact that the latter is much larger than the former, and
    sings bass,
But she is holding a piece of cardboard with two eyeholes in front
    of her face,
And in the world of opera this counts as an adequate disguise.
Also, there is the fact that everybody sings very healthily for a long
    time when he or she dies.
And furthermore, when you get two young lovers like Tristan and
    Isolde,
They are both forty pounds heavier than you expect, and fifty years
    older.
So please do not attempt to take me to Figaro or
    Lucia di Lammermoor:
I would relish sitting in a swamp being hit on the head with a
    hammer more.
I hope you enjoy your evening at La Bohème or the Magic Flute
    or Carmen.
Speaking for myself, I plan to renew acquaintance with several
    barmen.

Level 4

I am sorry to announce
that the 14.25 service to London Paddington
is delayed by approximately 34 minutes.
Please accept my sincere apologies for the delay
which is due to the late running of the train.

I know that some customers
question the sincerity of my apologies
due to the fact that I am a computer programme.
They should be advised
that my configuration incorporates a sincerity function
currently set at Level 4: 'Deeply Concerned'.

I am sorry to announce
that the 14.32 service to Bristol Parkway
is delayed by approximately seven hours
due to a signalling error at Slough
which has caused the train to be routed via Halifax.
Please accept my sincere apologies
for any inconvenience which this may cause.

Customers do not always realise
that high levels of sincerity
take an electronic toll.
A colleague of mine
whose function was set at Level 8:
'frantic but determined to carry on as normal'
crashed three times last week.
And not only my colleague, but –
excuse me a moment.

I am sorry to announce
that the 14.46 service
to Birmingham New Street
is delayed by approximately 45 minutes.
Please accept my sincere apologies for this delay
which is caused by the driver's lunch break.

Please stand well back from the platform.
The approaching train
is not scheduled to stop at this station
or indeed at any other,
so far as I can determine.
Ha-ha.

As you can see
my configuration
incorporates a sense of humour function.
This is currently set at Level 2:
'Good-natured banter'.

I am sorry to announce ...

STEVE TASANE

Drug Dog

"Britain's most sensitive nose stops sniffing"
The Independent

My handler says I found drugs out of pure enjoyment.
Fair cop. If it's pure I sniff it out with pure abandon,
and all that coke helps make me a springier Spaniel.
But now and then, right, I bite off more than I can handle –
like that bag of pure Colombian I made a dog's dinner.
So they made me have my stomach pumped and stuck me in a
rehab with those alcoholic Poodles, burnt-out Greyhounds
and doped-up Bulldogs. But, hey, you only live once,
and I've sent down some of Merseyside's most feared scallies.
So what's the big deal if I inhale occasionally
or do the odd line or two? I'm a sniffer dog for
God's sake! It's what I'm good at. It's not odd or
unprofessional. All dogs relax with a bit of blow.
And no, I'm not paranoid. But it's a bit of a coincidence how
they're making me 'retire' after that do with the White Doves
when me and the Alsatian got caught making puppy love.
We're beasts aren't we? That doesn't make us brutes.
I've always been a good dog, so where's the disrepute?
Eight years' clean service with no pension fund or bribes –
just a pat on the head when my neck's been on the line.
And why do you think our tails wag when we sniff out a stash?
We can't help ourselves, pal, we do it for the crack.
Not cos we're man's best friend – we do it out of habit.
And with this monkey on my back I've no time for chasing rabbits,
cos this massive lump of hash is the best I've ever tasted,
and if they're gonna make me go, I'm gonna go out wasted.

Roderic Vincent

Stop

I'd like to make a backup of my life
so that I can start again from here
if, for example, I piss off my wife
or sickness strikes the ones that I hold dear

or if I face a forced redundancy
or get caught with my mitten in the till
or simply sink with the economy
and reach a day when I can't pay the bill.

I'd keep it locked inside the biscuit tin
and just the knowledge it was safely hid
would guarantee that I will always win
free rein to do the things I never did.

I'd start by baking chocolate layer cake
then scoff the whole thing topped with triple cream.
I'd dive from high into a frozen lake
and take the shock without a single scream.

I'd spoon the peanut butter on my toast
and throw the jar in the uncycling bin
then phone up all my enemies and boast
how we could have a fight and I would win.

I'd pinch the bum of Susan in accounts
and then explain that feminism's done
while drinking gin in ludicrous amounts
and playing roulette with a loaded gun.

But when I found it all got out of hand
and hedonism wasn't all it's cracked
up to be but a sham, a phoney land
I'd reach out for the life I'd safely backed

up, hidden on the dusty kitchen shelf.
Then I'd restore my old life from the tin
slip on the garment of my former self
and live the way I do, devoid of sin.

Bloody Marvellous

I said, 'If we had but world enough and time
this coyness baby were no fucking crime.'

She said, 'Take your thieving finger off my knee
and don't get metaphysical with me.'

GAIL WHITE

Abelard, or Love Gone Wrong

My altered cat runs out the door
and rackets round the yard.
Because he'll be a stud no more,
I call him Abelard.

But when he meets a lady cat
with soft and yielding paws,
he doesn't quite remember that
he's not the man he was.

He climbs her back and bites her neck;
he recollects the game.
But still he meets a fatal check:
Results are not the same.

(How often, when romances end,
it puzzles cats and men
to know why last night's lady friend
will not step out again.)

Now other cats, with raucous glee,
cry out their mating song,
while Abelard sits home with me,
and wonders what went wrong.

JOHN WHITWORTH

The TUMP in Love

*TUMP stands for Totally Useless Male Poet according to Wendy Cope.
I am not a TUMP, Wendy says, because I have a car.*

Boy poets have these little beards
And most of them wear specs.
Though only technically weirds,
They mostly have these little beards,
The hairies overtop the sheareds,
They're terrible at sex,
Boy poets with their little beards
And unsuccessful necks.

Girl poets, quite contrariwise,
Are up for it in spades.
Though found in every shape and size,
Girl poets, all contrariwise,
Have burning, yearning bedroom eyes
And wear their hair in braids.
Girl poets (this is no surprise)
Are up for it in spades.

And, dearest reader, that is why
The girls avoid the tumps,
Preferring journalists and fly-
By-night directors, that is why
A versifier such as I
Must languish in the dumps.
The game's afoot, the stakes are high
And hearts (alas) are trumps.

God's Bounty

Rig the gratings, Mr Christian.
We are going to flog a banker.
Call the ratings, Mr Christian,
Now my soul begins to hanker
For the backbone of a banker.
Furl the sails and drop the anchor,
                              Mr Christian.

Raise the yardarm, Mr Christian.
We will hang a politician.
There's no pardon, Mr Christian
For a man of his condition.
When you hang a politician
It improves with repetition,
                              Mr Christian.

Roll the guns out, Mr Christian.
We can terminate the scumbags.
See, the sun's out, Mr Christian!
Let our bellies be our rumbags
When we terminate the scumbags.
Stuff their heads into our bumbags,
                              Mr Christian.

CHARLES WILKINSON

Not by Me

This poem was not written by me.
Should I send it packing, with its suitcase of shrill similes,
Its sly attempts at humour, its lines that do not scan,
Its hero with no story; its half-rhymes that clang.
I'll wave it on its way: its dead metaphors stink.

This poem was not written by me, I think.
Should I watch its fat stanzas waddle away
Or store a few images for another day,
And put line nine that's bright like a bang
In the left luggage locker or a security van.

But this poem was not written by me.
My work stopped rhyming in nineteen eighty-three.
There's a dead sheep in line thirteen.
It could be a symbol, but where has it been?
It could have been rural or belonged to God,

And I'd like to get rid of it but that's proving hard
Because this poem does not belong to me.
Its rhythms are irregular. I should show it the door
Or at least put it away in the bottom drawer,
And wait until it stinks.

I hope that no one thinks the last line was too short
And that I have no control over my craft
Because this poem was not written by me.
It's just stopped rhyming; it hasn't got my voice.
Yet it still keeps coming. I haven't got a choice:

Every time the verse tries to wriggle free
There's a metre thumping that's not to do with me.
I'll open the sad suitcase, and let the rhymes fall out.
I'll let its words wither, for there is no doubt
This poem was not written by me.

These words that spin across the page
Seem to have come from a different age
Where the rhymes pop one by one
And the rhythm kicks like the dead and gone.
The beat is the beat of rigor mortis

And now my only thought is –
That this poem does not belong to me.
That it's still being written is a tragedy.
Its words are emerging from a pale mist.
It hasn't got a plot; it has no twist,

But every time I try to bring it to an end
It just keeps going with its blend
Of five-line stanzas and a way with metaphor
That's highly ineffective or been used before.
Yes, there's no doubt that it's been a flop.

I don't know where it comes from but really it must stop.
So I won't dally; this stanza is a crime.
Though there is the bonanza of three extra lines
And one fairly good example of internal rhyme,
I don't want the credit for I know without a doubt
(And I don't want to threaten, I don't want to shout,
So I'll just say this quietly, and then let you be):
This poem, yes, this poem is not by me.

THE POETS

Amanda Baker is an author/performance poet who has two anti-romantic novels published and recently launched *Eleanor and the Dragons of Death* for junior readers. Daughter of a Guyanese mother and British father she lives in Northumberland with her two youngest daughters.

Melissa Balmain's poems have appeared in *The Spectator, Light Quarterly, The Chimaera, Measure,* and elsewhere. She writes magazine articles and teaches writing in Rochester, NY, where she and her husband are raising two children and two jealous cats.

David Bateman, a Liverpool Kentish poet and story-writer, was Liverpool Poetry Slam Champion 2007. He teaches creative writing, mostly in mental health contexts. Collections: *Curse Of The Killer Hedge* (IRON Press), *A Homage To Me* (Driftwood) and *The Utter Glamour* (Reprobate). He edited *The Dead Good Poets Society: The Book* (Headland).

Pauline Beaumont lives in Northumberland with the youngest of her six children and works part time at Newcastle University. She likes to write at the kitchen table while simultaneously baking, so there's always something good at the end of the process. Her inspirations include Ogden Nash and Harry Graham.

Jerome Betts is from Herefordshire but now works in Devon. His verse has appeared in many publications, including *Haltwhistle Quarterly, Pennine Platform, Phoenix, Poetry Nottingham, Staple, The Guardian* and *Westwords,* mostly under the name 'G.E. Rome', as did a parodic sequence, *Travails With A Skeleton,* in the *Outposts* series.

Margaret Bevan mainly writes short stories but has been an occasional versifier for years. She says the most recent in "my brief list of triumphs" was a poem in *Bards in the Bog,* "the Shetland project that put poetry in public toilets."

Christine Bousfield is a retired lecturer in literature and psychoanalysis, interested in the unconscious in language and music. Her poetry is widely published in magazines, anthologies and on CD, and she performs (often with music) in festivals throughout the UK.

Diana Brodie was born in New Zealand and lives in Cambridge. Her poems have appeared in *Agenda, Smiths Knoll, The Rialto, Poetry News, The Interpreter's House, Poetry Nottingham, Borderlines* and

Weyfarers, and on websites. Competition successes include a shortlisting for the Hamish Canham Prize. She has completed a first collection.

Helen Burke has written/performed poetry for 30 years; competition wins include: Manchester Poetry Comp, Devon and Dorset, Suffolk, Sheffield Poetstars, Ilkley Performance Prize. Her collection *Zuzu's Petals* was launched at her one woman show at Edinburgh and her new collection will be launched at Edinburgh Festival next year. She also writes plays.

Marianne Burton was awarded a mentorship by the poetry magazine *Smiths Knoll,* and the resulting pamphlet *The Devil's Cut* was a Poetry Book Society choice. She's widely published in the UK, US and South Africa, and her first full collection is forthcoming from Seren Books.

Kevin Cadwallender lives in Edinburgh and has books published by IRON Press, Dogeater Press, Smokestack Books, Calder Wood Press and Red Squirrel Press. *Baz Uber Alles* was recently released on Black Lantern Music and his next book is *Defragmenting Sappho*, transcreations of the poetry of Sappho.

Diane Cockburn was born in Magherafelt in Northern Ireland. Her first pamphlet collection *Under Surveillance* is published by Vane Women Press. She roams the countryside in gigantic earrings looking for Bryan Ferry and Twiglets. Her collection *Electric Mermaid* is nearing completion.

Wendy Cope was a primary school teacher until the publication of her first book of poems, *Making Cocoa for Kingsley Amis*, in 1986. *Two Cures for Love*, a selection from her first three books, appeared in 2008. *Family Values* (2011) is her fourth collection.

Andy Croft's most recent collections are *Ghost Writer, Sticky*, and *Three Men on the Metro* (with Bill Herbert and Paul Summers). Edited anthologies include *Red Sky at Night* (with Adrian Mitchell), *North by North East* (with Cynthia Fuller) and *Not Just a Game* (with Sue Dymoke).

Barbara Cumbers lives in London with a husband and two cats. She has had poems in various magazines including *Acumen, Poetry London, Smiths Knoll* and *Staple*. She is currently working on a first collection.

Liz Dean is an ex-pat northerner who now writes and edits books in London. Her poems reflect on pleasures old and new: tarot, jazz, eating and relationships. Recent poems have appeared in *Obsessed With Pipework*, *14 magazine* and *South Bank Poetry*.

Josh Ekroy's poems have appeared in *Smiths Knoll*, *The SHOp*, and others. In 2009, he won first prize in the Bedford Competition, was commended in the Poetry London Competition and gained third prize in the Keats-Shelley Competition. He lives in London.

Sylvia Forrest's collection, *Waltzing off from Hand me Downs* was published by Diamond Twig Press and demonstrates her quirky imagination. Her poem, *Fish Shop Person* was on the Tyneside Metro system. Her poetry comes from childhood loss, wild landscape, music, clothes, food, travel and learning.

Kate Fox is a poet in residence on Radio 4's *Saturday Live*, writing topical, funny poems. She performs her work widely: everywhere from Aldeburgh Poetry Festival to the Southbank Centre. Her one woman stand-up and poetry show *Kate Fox News* has toured to the Edinburgh Fringe Festival and nationally.

Linda France's latest poetry collection is *You are Her* (Arc Publications 2010), named after a faded information board on Hadrian's Wall. She has also written plays and prose, and worked on numerous collaborations in stone, wood, glass, steel, enamel, ceramics.

Janis Freegard was born in South Shields, but has lived in New Zealand most of her life. Her poetry has been published in *AUP New Poets 3* (Auckland University Press) and many poetry magazines, including *Poetry NZ* and *The North*.

Nandita Ghose is a poet, playwright and artist. Magazine publication includes *Magma*, *The Wolf*, and *South Bank Poetry*. Shortlisted for the Bridport, winner of an Edinburgh Fringe Award for funniest poem, she performs widely, including her recent poetry performance and installations, *Kitchen Martyr* and *Mrs Whippy Serves it Up*.

Paul Groves featured in *Poetry Introduction 3* (Faber, 1975). He received an Eric Gregory Award in 1976. His collections *Academe* (1988), *Ménage à Trois* (1995), *Eros and Thanatos* (1999), *Wowsers* (2002), and *Qwerty* (2008) are published by Seren Books. Starborn brought out the autobiographical *Country Boy* in 2007.

Gill Hands, a poet, writer and artist living in Cumbria has published two collections: *Internet Love Slut* and *Rilke Tattoo*. Her poetry has been called 'witty and surreal' and she has performed at numerous venues as diverse as The Poetry Café and Glastonbury Festival.

Oz Hardwick is a York-based writer, photographer and occasional musician. He has published a number of books, most recently the poetry collection *The Illuminated Dreamer* (Oversteps, 2010). He is programme leader for English and Writing at Leeds Trinity University College.

John Hegley, North London born and based, a regular in the North East, running potato-drawing workshops in Sunderland, and much poetry – encouraged by Connie Pickard in Newcastle's Morden Tower. Selecting the three pieces here-in was a happy process, undertaken in the Live Theatre bar with Eileen Jones and her twin sister, Kate.

W. N. Herbert, Professor of Poetry and Creative Writing at Newcastle University, was born in Dundee, and educated at Brasenose College, Oxford. His last 5 collections, with Bloodaxe Books, have won numerous accolades. Shortlisted twice for the T S Eliot prize and twice for the Saltire, he's gained 3 PBS Recommendations, and 3 Scottish Arts Council Awards

Joan Johnston is a writing tutor/facilitator in further education and in a women's health project. She's worked as a writer in schools, hospitals, prisons and with homeless people and elderly people. Two collections: *What you Want*, (Diamond Twig) and *Orange for the Sun*, (Dogeater). Awarded Hawthornden Fellowship in 2000.

Eileen Jones writes poetry and plays. She had a short play produced by the New Writing North 'Emerge' programme in 2006 and has had poems published in *Jackie, The Guardian, The North, Other Poetry* and in several anthologies.

Julie Kane teaches English and Creative Writing at Northwestern State University of Louisiana. Her 2003 collection, *Rhythm & Booze*, was a winner of the National Poetry Series and a finalist for the Poets' Prize. Her most recent, *Jazz Funeral*, won the 2009 Donald Justice Poetry Prize.

Janina Aza Karpinska completed an M.A. in Creative Writing & Personal Development at Sussex University and is currently running writing workshops in local shops and businesses. She has had poems published online and in a Macmillan's children's anthology and won first prize in a Cannon Poets open poetry competition.

Valerie Laws has current residencies at a London Pathology museum and Newcastle University and specialises in sci-art installations and commissions, including *Quantum Sheep*. She recently featured in BBC2's

Why Poetry Matters. Four of her eight books are poetry, published by Peterloo Poets and IRON Press.

Joan Lennon lives in Fife and has four sons. She writes poetry in between children's books, and has had poems published in magazines, and in anthologies such as *Scotland's Weather* and *The Thing That Mattered Most.*

Sarah Macleod was born in South Wales, grew up in Scotland, then Cornwall, and now lives near Oxford. She has always written poetry, but a serious illness in 2006 prompted her to write more. She has a son, daughter, and three grandchildren.

Gerda Mayer, born in Czechoslovakia, came to England at the age of 11 in 1939. She has published several collections of verse, one of which has received a Poetry Book Society recommendation, and her poems have been widely anthologised. Her autobiographical prose vignette, *Prague Winter,* was published in 2005 (Hearing Eye).

Ian McMillan has been a freelance writer, performer and broadcaster for thirty years; he's currently working with The Ian McMillan Orchestra and the cartoonist Tony Husband and presenting *The Verb* on BBC Radio 3. He's a busy boy!

Allison McVety's collection, *The Night Trotsky Came to Stay* (Smith/Doorstop), was shortlisted for the Forward Best First CollectionPrize 2008. Her poems have appeared in *The Times* and *PN Review* and on BBC radio. She was shortlisted in the MMU Poetry Prize 2008. Her second collection, *Miming Happiness* (Smith/Doorstop), was published in 2010.

Hilary Menos was born in Luton in 1964, studied PPE at Oxford, and worked as a journalist before moving to Devon where she now runs an organic farm with her husband and four sons. Her first collection, *Berg,* was shortlisted for the Forward Poetry Best First Collection 2010.

Peter Mortimer was his mum's favourite poet and has a mantlepiece whose dusting is made easier by the lack of poetic awards. More than 20 plays and a dozen books have appeared, mainly to a clamorous indifference. He lives in Cullercoats where twice daily tides are taken as read.

Sean O'Brien is Professor of Creative Writing at Newcastle University. His six poetry collections have all won awards, most recently *The Drowned Book* (Picador), which won the 2007 Forward and T S Eliot Prizes. A new collection, *November,* is due out in 2011. His first novel, *Afterlife,* was published in 2009.

Rennie Parker has published with Flambard and Shoestring; her next collection, *Borderville*, is due from Shoestring in 2011. She has also published criticism, and edited two anthologies.

Pauline Plummer, born in Liverpool, has lived in the North East for 28 years – as well as many other places. Her poems are bluesy rather than comic, so this is a diversion. Her most recent full collection was *Demon Straightening* (IRON Press); *Bint* is due next year from Red Squirrel Press.

Jacob Polley was born in Carlisle in 1975. His first collection, *The Brink*, was short-listed for the T S Eliot Prize, and his second, *Little Gods*, was a PBS Recommendation. He won the 2010 Somerset Maugham Award for his novel, *Talk of the Town*. His work is published by Picador.

June Portlock lives in Gateshead. Her poems have been published in a wide variety of magazines and in anthologies and she has won or been runner up in many competitions. Her collection, *Broken Biscuits* was published by Diamond Twig Press. She has self published a novel, *The Colour of Pegs*.

Jeff Price tries to write universal poems but ends up always writing about himself. He is obsessed by his failing body, his daughters' failure to realise that he is always right and he likes to vent his frustrations with the world through his poetry.

D. A. Prince lives in Leicestershire, and her poetry – including light verse – appears regularly in a wide range of magazines. Her first full-length collection, *Nearly the Happy Hour*, was published by Happen*Stance* Press in 2008.

Laura Quigley lives in South West England and writes mainly for performance without making much money yet. But she's had some successes with poetry and short stories while bringing up two kids and working for a living.

Joyce Reed is a retired music teacher and writer with several self published collections of short stories and poems. Recently she set up the successful 'Marple' writing competition, which in 2010, was for Poetry. When not writing she enjoys gardening.

Guy Russell was born in Chatham and now works for the Open University in Milton Keynes. He has had recent work in *Brace* (Comma Press), *Reflections from Mirror City* (Tongue in Chic) and *Troubles Swapped For Something Fresh* (Salt Publishing).

Mo Ryan is also Maureen Ryan, an Anglican priest. She has published over 300 academic papers, sermons, meditations and worthy poems, but when holiness hangs heavy, and the moon is full, Mo Ryan appears, cackling, to write saucy novels and silly poems.

Gwen Seabourne was born in Abergavenny and raised in Sunderland. She researches medieval legal history and writes poetry on historical and modern themes. Her poems have appeared in magazines, on Radio 4, and she has performed at the Bristol International Poetry Festival.

Murray Shelmerdine's first collection of poems, *Sermons of Sedition* was published by Nettle Press in 2008. His poems have appeared in various magazines. His short stories have been published in *Crimewave* and in two recent anthologies. He produces and presents *Poetry Now and Then* on Resonance FM.

Sim Smailes is a Yorkshireman living in Essex and an ex-primary school teacher who is now a crime analyst. He has enjoyed writing poetry since he was a teenager and humorous poetry is his favourite genre.

Natalie Smith has a Creative Writing and Literature Diploma from the OU. Her favourite poets are Pablo Neruda and John Cooper Clarke. She is currently working on a short story anthology, as part of Exeter University's South West Writers' Mentoring Project.

Paul Summers was born in Blyth, Northumberland, in 1967. Publications include: *Three Men on the Metro* (Five Leaves 2009), *Big Bella's Dirty Cafe* (Dogeater 2006), *Last Bus* (IRON Press 1998). He has performed all over the world, co-edited *Billy Liar* and *Liar Republic*, and written for TV, film, radio, theatre and mixed-media projects.

Joy C. Swan, a member of Hexham Writers Group, likes reading and writing poetry which has rhyme and rhythm and is readily accessible. Runner up in a recent NAWG poetry competition, she's had other competition successes and performs her poetry at 'Lamplight' Open Mic sessions in Stanley and elsewhere. She also writes short stories and scripts.

Michael Swan works in English language teaching and applied linguistics. His poems are published widely, and have won prizes, including *The Times* Stephen Spender competition for his translated version of Rilke's *Orpheus, Eurydike, Hermes*. First collection is *When They Come For You* (Frogmore Press 2003); he is seeking a publisher for his second.

Steve Tasane combines biting political satire with playful children's poetry. Anthologised by Hodder, Walker Books and Oxfam, he prefers live performance – anywhere from Glastonbury Festival to London's Barbican. He produces poetry films specifically for *You Tube*, and has an exciting website.

Roderic Vincent is a Chartered Psychologist living in London. His stories have been short-listed for prizes including the Bridport Prize and the Aesthetica Annual 2009. He is currently submitting his second novel to literary agents and publishers.

Gail White is the author of *Easy Marks* (David Robert Books) and *The Accidental Cynic* (Prospero's World Press). She is the subject of an essay in the web journal *Mezzo Cammin*. Her poetry has appeared in *The Spectator* and *Lighten Up Online*. She lives in Breaux Bridge, Louisiana, with her husband and cats.

John Whitworth says he is one of those fattish, baldish, backward-looking, provincial poets in which England is so rich. His ninth collection, *Being the Bad Guy,* was published by Peterloo in 2007. Les Murray likes it. His *Writing Poetry* (A & C Black), 'one of those how-to books' has run to a second edition.

Charles Wilkinson was born in Birmingham in 1950. His collection, *The Snowman and Other Poems* was published by IRON Press in 1987; London Magazine Editions published *The Pain Tree and Other Stories* in 2000.

Acknowledgements

Amanda Baker SNAIL LOVE reprinted by permission of the poet.
Melissa Balmain FLUFFY WEIGHS IN ON THE BABY reprinted by permission of the poet. First published in *Light Quarterly 2007*.
David Bateman CURSE OF THE KILLER HEDGE, from *Curse of the Killer Hedge* published by IRON Press 1996. Reprinted by permission of the poet.
Pauline Beaumont JOBS BLOODBATH AT GOLDMAN SACHS reprinted by permission of the poet.
Jerome Betts QUEEN OF GREENS reprinted by permission of the poet.
Margaret Bevan MARY MARY and MOAN, MOAN, MOAN, MOAN, MOAN reprinted by permission of the poet.
Christine Bousfield MINIMED 508 INSULIN PUMP reprinted by permission of the poet.
Diana Brodie A CHOICE OF HANDS reprinted by permission of the poet. First published in *The Rialto 67*.
Helen Burke MY WILD MOTHER reprinted by permission of the poet.
Marianne Burton VIEWING AT THE NATIONAL reprinted by permission of the poet. First published *Smiths Knoll 38* then *The Devil's Cut* (Smiths Knoll pamphlet 2007).
Kevin Cadwallender COLOURING IN GUERNICA from *Colouring in Guernica* reprinted by permission of Red Squirrel Press 2007.
Diane Cockburn SUPERMAN'S LEMMING first published in *The Big Anthology*, University of Northumbria, 2005, reprinted by permission of the poet.
Wendy Cope A POEM ON THE THEME OF HUMOUR from *If I Don't Know* reprinted by permission of Faber and Faber Ltd. ©Wendy Cope 2001.
Andy Croft OUTFACED from *Comrade Laughter*, Flambard Press 2004, reprinted by permission of Flambard Press. First published in *Acumen 45*.
Barbara Cumbers GLOBBERWORMY reprinted by permission of the poet. First published in *Smiths Knoll 41*.
Liz Dean CONSOLED reprinted by permission of the poet. First published in *Obsessed With Pipework 50*.
Josh Ekroy KAFKA'S RECIPE FOR BOILED CABBAGE first published in *The Interpreter's House 33*, then in *The Sandhopper Lover and Other Stories and Poems* (Cinnamon Press anthology). VICROSSLOO STATION PLC first prize winner, Strokestown Satirical Poem Competition 2008. Both reprinted by permission of the poet.
Sylvia Forrest RE-CREATION from *Waltzing off from Hand me Downs* (Diamond Twig Press 1997), reprinted by permission of Diamond Twig Press. First published in Foyle Street Writers anthology.
Kate Fox SMALL GIRLFRIENDS and BEING SYLVIA PLATH from *Why not I too?* (Zebra Publishing 2009), reprinted by permission of Zebra Publishing.
Linda France ON THE CIRCLE LINE from *Red* (Bloodaxe Books 1992), reprinted by permission of the poet. MRS FOONER IS SPIFTY from *You are Her* (Arc 2010), reprinted by permission of Arc Publications.
Janis Freegard PLEASE RUSH ME reprinted by permission of the poet.
Nandita Ghose A QUESTION OF FROM reprinted by permission of the poet.
Paul Groves GREENLAND LITERATI from *Qwerty* (Seren Books 2008), reprinted by

permission of Seren Books. First published in *The North*, 2004.

Gill Hands, Devil's Advocate from *Rilke Tattoo* (Wild Women Press 2006), reprinted by permission of Wild Women Press.

Oz Hardwick Elvis Lives Next Door reprinted by permission of the poet. First published in *The Connecticut Review*, Spring 2007.

John Hegley A Waltz in Dunstable Downs, An Ending of the Re-offending and Art in Melbourne reprinted by permission of the poet.

W. N. Herbert Answermachine from *Cabaret McGonagall* (Bloodaxe Books 1996) reprinted by permission of Bloodaxe Books. To a Moussaka reprinted by permission of the poet.

Joan Johnston What You Want from *What You Want* (Diamond Twig Press 1999), reprinted by permission of Diamond Twig Press.

Eileen Jones In County Hall first published in *Other Poetry* and in *Miracles and Clockwork* (*The Best of Other Poetry Series Two*).

Julie Kane Plea Bargain reprinted by permission of the poet. First published in *Light Quarterly*.

Janina Aza Karpinska It's a Jungle Out There reprinted by permission of the poet.

Valerie Laws Wonderbra! from *Quantum Sheep* (Peterloo Poets 2006), reprinted by permission of the poet.

Joan Lennon Since I have had Children reprinted by permission of the poet. First published in *Spectrum 6*.

Sarah Macleod The Day Kitty Knitted an Orgasm reprinted by permission of the poet. First published in Faringdon online competition anthology, *Cool and Quirky*, by Elixir Press.

Gerda Mayer The Misanthrope's Baby Poem, from *Bernini's Cat* (IRON Press 1999). Also first prize winner in *Spectator* competition, 23rd April, 2005. Reprinted by permission of the poet.

Ian McMillan Praise Poem for Yorkshire Puddings reprinted by permission of the poet.

Allison McVety Offspring reprinted from her collection *Miming Happiness* (Smith/Doorstop 2010), reprinted by permission of Smith/Doorstop. First published in *Smiths Knoll 43*.

Hilary Menos Off My Trolley from *Berg* (Seren Books 2010). Reprinted by permission of Seren Books. First published in *Mslexia 30*.

Peter Mortimer Read a Book Every day from *I Married the Angel of the North* (Five Leaves Publications 2002), reprinted by permission of Five Leaves Publications.

Sean O'Brien Three Facetious Poems from *The Drowned Book*, reprinted by permission of Pan MacMillan, London. © Sean O'Brien 2007.

Rennie Parker The Plaque, the Chandelier, the Box of Tricks reprinted by permission of the poet.

Pauline Plummer At the Greengrocer's from *Romeo's Café* (Paranoia Press 1992), reprinted by permission of the poet.

Jacob Polley The Gulls and from Definitions for the Wife from *The Brink*, reprinted by permission of Pan MacMillan, London. © Jacob Polley 2003.

June Portlock Dear Milkman from *Broken Biscuits* (Diamond Twig Press 1997), reprinted by permission of Diamond Twig Press.

Jeff Price Ten Things I Have Observed in the ASDA Car Park in Gosforth reprinted by permission of the poet. First published in *The Book of Ten* (Zebra Publishing 2009).

D. A. Prince A Pig, Satisfied reprinted by permission of the poet. First published in *Lighten Up Online 10*.

Laura Quigley Greetings Card reprinted by permission of the poet.

Joyce Reed Melamine Dreams and A Place in the Sun reprinted by permission of the poet. Melamine Dreams first published in a Forward Press regional anthology 2009.

Guy Russell Everybody Knows and Keats Goes to the Workshop reprinted by permission of the poet. Everybody Knows first published in *The Rialto*. Keats Goes to the Workshop first published in *The Interpreter's House 18*.

Mo Ryan Dear William and Saga Love reprinted by permission of the poet. Dear William first published in *The SHOp*.

Gwen Seabourne Snake Charm Offensive and Regressional reprinted by permission of the poet. Snake Charm Offensive was a winner of a BBC Wildlife Poetry award and first published in *BBC Wildlife Magazine* October 2004 under the pen-name Caroline Otterson. Regressional first published in *Snakeskin* poetry e-zine issue 159.

Murray Shelmerdine The Garden reprinted by permission of the poet. First published in *Magma 8*.

Sim Smailes Dead Parrot Limerick reprinted by permission of the poet.

Natalie Smith A Farewell Note from Mummy reprinted by permission of the poet.

Paul Summers fossil from *big bella's dirty café* (Dogeater Press 2006), reprinted by permission of the poet.

Joy C. Swan Erotica to Potica, reprinted by permission of the poet.

Michael Swan Opera and Level 4 reprinted by permission of the poet. Opera first published in *The Spectator* May 2000 (competition winner). Level 4 first published in *Dreamcatcher 22*.

Steve Tasane Drug Dog reprinted by permission of the poet.

Roderic Vincent Stop and Bloody Marvellous reprinted by permission of the poet.

Gail White Abelard, or Love Gone Wrong reprinted by permission of the poet. First published in *Light Quarterly*.

John Whitworth God's Bounty and Tump in Love reprinted by permission of the poet. Tump in Love first published in *Quadrant*.

Charles Wilkinson Not by Me reprinted by permission of the poet.

GERDA MAYER

The Misanthrope's Baby Poem

I look at them, if look I must:
I view them with benign disgust.

I see them with disguised dismay;
And do I covet them? – No way!

My own would have improved the nation.
Yours make for overpopulation.

Parental Pride, do not suppose
I like them much beyond their toes.

I very cheerfully dispense
With whiffs of their incontinence.

They have one single merit – that's
Being a substitute for cats.

Have they a sex? The only clues
Are puky pinks and bilious blues.

What is their weather? Wet and windy.
Their yowling makes a dismal shindy.

They're boring, bawling, bandy, bald.
I straight forget what they are called.

How's Baby? Whey – and pudding-faced;
Uncalled for proof that you've embraced.

I'd not have doubted it. A letter –
French – dropped my way would have done better.

For every Jack, for every Janet,
Commiserations, luckless Planet!

IAN MCMILLAN

Praise Poem for Yorkshire Puddings

Light brown moon in a gravy sky
Round O of delight on a big white plate
Floppy as a vest if you get 'em out early;
Hard as a wall if you get 'em out late!

Alchemy of eggs and milk and flour
Aesthetically gorgeous in a kitchenful of steam
Cultural symbol with enduring power;
Perfect as a sunset, elusive as a dream.

All in the wrist to get the air in the batter
As the shattered eggshells lie crushed like martyrs
As they wait to grace your Sunday platter:
The Yorkshire Pudding is the Queen of Starters!

My blood is racing and my heart is thudding
At the thought of this dinnertime's Yorkshire Pudding!